Ex Libris

Designed and produced by Marquand Books, Inc.
Quality printing and binding by Tien Wah Press Pte, Ltd.,
977 Bukit Timah Road, Singapore 2158

Efforts have been made to find the copyright
holders of material used in this publication. We apologize
for any omissions or errors and will be pleased to include
the appropriate acknowledgments in future editions.

Lyrics from "Professor Hauptmann's Performing Dogs"
© 1975 Jerry Leiber Music & Mike Stoller Music.
All rights reserved. Used by permission.
Excerpt from the Mary McGrory column by Mary McGrory.
Copyright © 1990 by Universal Press Syndicate.
Reprinted with permission. All rights reserved.
Excerpt from Harry J. Mooney, *How to Train Your Own Dogs*,
Saalfield Publishing, © 1909.

ISBN 0-87701-844-8

Distributed in Canada by Raincoast Books
112 East 3rd Avenue, Vancouver, B.C. V5T1C8

1 3 5 7 9 10 8 6 4 2

Chronicle Books
275 Fifth Street, San Francisco, California 94103

ELITE STUDIO.
1177 GRANVILLE ST.

Snapshot Keepsake Book
Instructions

If necessary, trim your pet's snapshots down to
the size of this card ($5'' \times 4''$), and slip each one
into a pocket page. A spot of glue or tape on the
back of the snapshot will hold it in place.

There are four pocket pages in this book.

Put Your Dog on the Cover

You can put your dog's snapshot on the cover of
this book. Trim your photograph to a two-inch
circle. Attach this to the recessed area with rub-
ber cement, white glue, double-stick tape or gluestick
adhesive. (Do not trim or cut self-developing instant
snapshots. They may contain caustic chemicals.)

**Slip this card out
of this pocket page
for your
Snapshot Keepsake
Book instructions.**

My Dog

A Snapshot
Keepsake Book

MICHELE DURKSON CLISE

CHRONICLE BOOKS
San Francisco

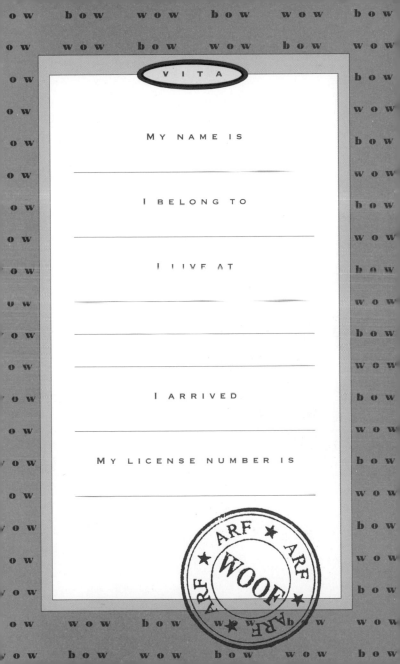

VITA

My name is

I belong to

I live at

I arrived

My license number is

ARF · ARF · WOOF · ARF · ARF

FAMILY

THE ONE ABSOLUTELY UNSELFISH FRIEND
THAT MAN CAN HAVE IN THIS SELFISH WORLD,
THE ONE THAT NEVER DESERTS HIM, THE
ONE THAT NEVER PROVES UNGRATEFUL OR
TREACHEROUS, IS HIS DOG.

—*George G. Vest*

My Life Story

_____

_____

_____

_____

_____

_____

_____

_____

_____

_____

_____

_____

_____

_____

Bow - Wow

Alley

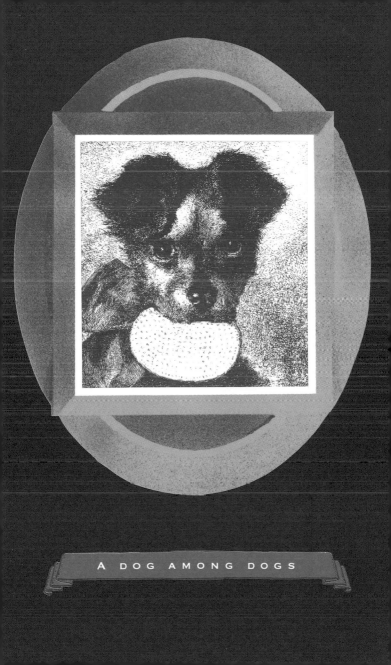

A DOG AMONG DOGS

THINGS I DO
BUT SHOULDN'T

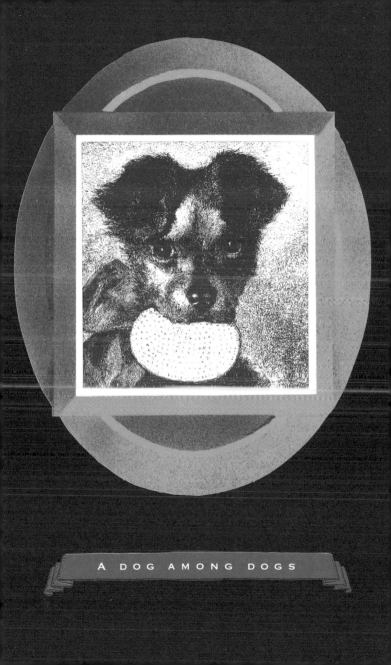

A DOG AMONG DOGS

THINGS I DO BUT SHOULDN'T

THINGS I DON'T DO BUT SHOULD

Dogs would make much more satisfactory pets if,
instead of whimpering when a thunderstorm breaks
in the middle of the night,
they would tiptoe in and close the windows.

—*Anonymous*

speak sit bark drop run jump fet
rollover heel speak sit bark dro
ump fetch catch rollover heel spe
bark drop run jump fet
er heel speak sits ba
atch rollover he
ump fetch ca
k drop ru
speak li
rollo
ump
bar
er h
ch
ng
k
s

SO ALL THE LITTLE DOGS RAN AS FAS

Sports

_____
_____
_____
_____
_____
_____
_____

Hobbies

If you are going to have a dog,
first have a good dog; second, train it to be useful.
It takes a little trouble to train a dog, maybe, but you will
find that it more than pays in the end. It will give you a
broader sympathy with the animal world, and that
includes your fellowmen.

—*Harry J. Mooney*

PROFESSOR HAUPTMANN'S PERFORMING DOGS
PROFESSOR HAUPTMANN'S MIRACULOUS DOGS
JUGGLERS AND ACROBATS DRESSED UP LIKE CLOWNS
DOGS IN TUXEDOS AND SWANK EVENING GOWNS ...
ONE RIDES A PONY AND CARRIES A PURSE
ONE IS ON ROLLER SKATES DRESSED LIKE A NURSE
A DOG IN A DERBY IS DOING A DANCE
A MUTT IN RED SUSPENDERS KEEPS ON LOSING HIS PANTS ...

PROFESSOR HAUPTMANN'S PERFORMING DOGS
PROFESSOR HAUPTMANN'S SPECTACULAR DOGS
WATCH THEM DO SOMERSAULTS, CARTWHEELS AND SPRINGS
SEE THEM CAVORTING AND JUMPING THROUGH RINGS
BREATHTAKING STUNTS THAT AMAZE AND SURPRISE
FEATS OF SKILL AND DARING RIGHT BEFORE YOUR OWN EYES ...
ONE PLAYS THE FIFE AND ONE BEATS THE DRUM
ONE WAVES THE FLAG WHILE HE WALKS AND CHEWS GUM ...

—*Jerry Leiber*

THE MORE I SEE OF MEN,
THE BETTER I LIKE MY DOG.
—Frederick the Great

Dogmatism is the maturity of puppyism.
—*Douglas Jerrold*

IF A DOG'S PRAYERS WERE ANSWERED,
BONES WOULD RAIN FROM THE SKY.

— *Proverb*

Favorite Foods

Dogs, bless them, operate on the premise that
human beings are fragile and require incessant
applications of affection and reassurance. The
random lick of the hand and the furry chin
draped over the instep are calculated to let the
shaky owner know that a friend is nearby.

—*Mary McGrory*

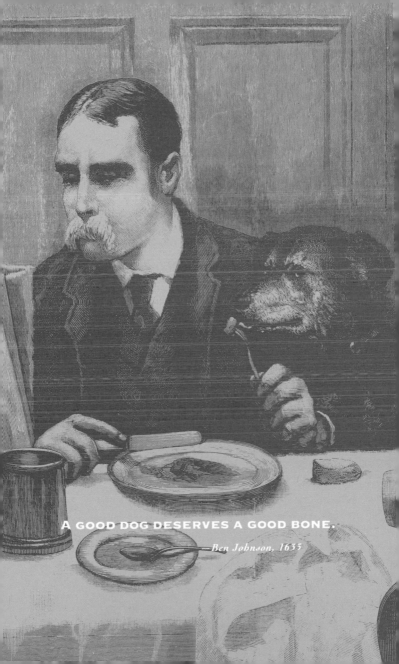

A GOOD DOG DESERVES A GOOD BONE.

—*Ben Johnson, 1633*

Bum

He's a little dog, with a stubby tail,
and a moth-eaten coat of tan,
And his legs are short, of the wabbly sort:
I doubt if they ever ran;
And he howls at night, while in broad daylight
he sleeps like a bloomin' log,
And he likes the food of the gutter breed;
he's a most irregular dog.

I call him Bum, and in total sum
he's all that his name implies,
For he's just a tramp with a highway stamp
that culture cannot disguise;
And his friends, I've found, in the streets abound,
be they urchins or dogs or men;
Yet he sticks to me with a fiendish glee;
It is truly beyond my ken.

. . .

So my good old pal, my irregular dog,
my flea-bitten, stub-tailed friend,
Has become a part of my very heart,
to be cherished till life-time's end:
And on Judgment Day, if I take the way
that leads where the righteous meet,
If my dog is barred by the heavenly guard
we'll both of us brave the heat!

— *W. Dayton Wedgefarth*

'TIS SWEET TO HEAR THE WATCH-DOG'S HONEST BARK
BAY DEEP-MOUTH'D WELCOME AS WE DRAW NEAR HOME;
'TIS SWEET TO KNOW THERE IS AN EYE WILL MARK
OUR COMING, AND LOOK BRIGHTER WHEN WE COME.
—*Lord Byron*

THE GREAT PLEASURE OF A DOG IS THAT YOU MAY
MAKE A FOOL OF YOURSELF WITH HIM AND NOT ONLY
WILL HE NOT SCOLD YOU, BUT HE WILL MAKE
A FOOL OF HIMSELF TOO.

—*Samuel Butler*

NO ONE APPRECIATES THE VERY SPECIAL GENIUS OF
YOUR CONVERSATION AS A DOG DOES.

—*Christopher Morley*

The best thing about a man is his dog.
—French proverb

Buddies

DOGS

E SCAMP REX FIDO REX MUFFIN SPOT SKIPPER MAJOR
NNY HOBO TIPPY SPOT SKIPPER MAJOR SCOTTY PENNY H
KI MAGGIE SCAMP PIERRE FIFI GINGER LADY SUKI MA

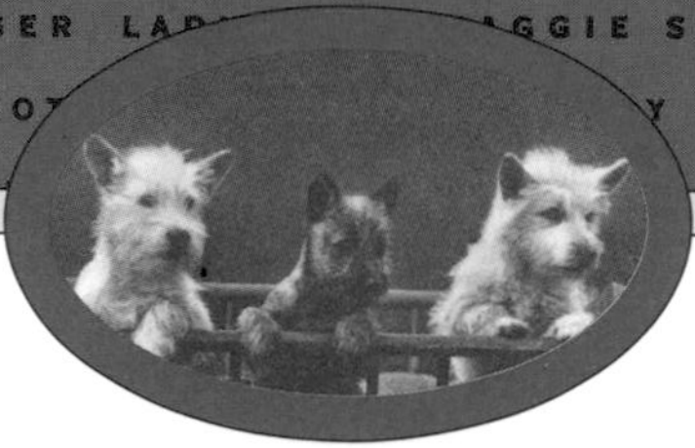

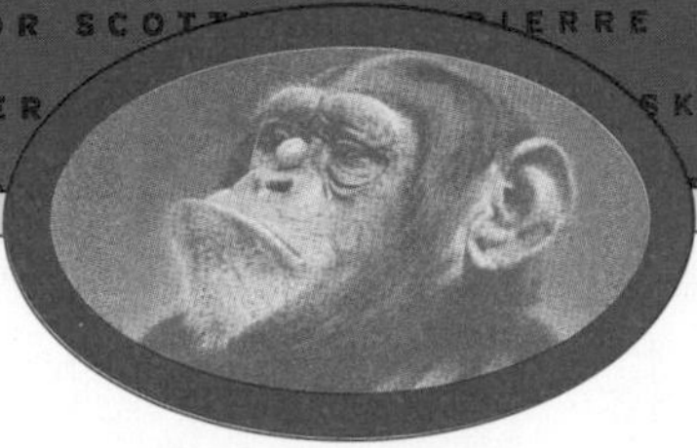

Friends

OTHER SPECIES

Dogs around the world

Chinese	**Italian**
gou	*cane*
Dutch	**Japanese**
hond	*inu*
Finnish	**Persian**
koira	*sag*
French	**Spanish**
chien	*perro*
German	**Swahili**
hund	*mbwa*
Greek	**Thai**
skilos	*rmah*
Hindi	**Turkish**
kutta	*kopek*
Icelandic	**Yugoslavian**
hundur	*pas*

DOG WITH THE PENSIVE HAZEL EYES,
SHAGGY COAT, OR FEET OF TAN,
WHAT DO YOU THINK WHEN YOU LOOK SO WISE
INTO THE FACE OF YOUR FELLOW, MAN?
—*W. C. Olmsted*

Medical Records

Vet's name and telephone

_____

_____

_____

Allergies

_____

_____

Special medications

_____

_____

_____

_____

_____

Vaccinations

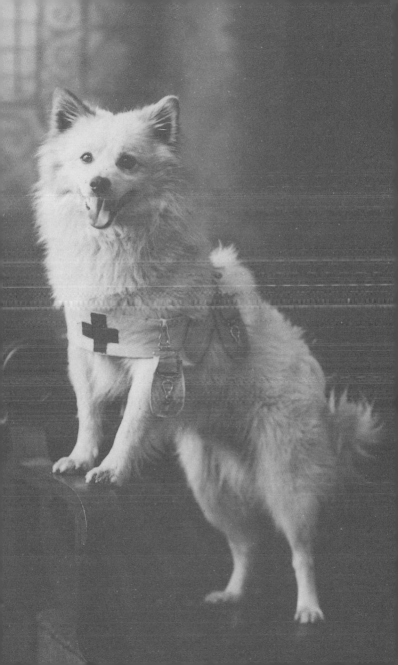

LOVE ME, LOVE MY DOG.

—*Saint Bernard of Clairvaux*

Sitter's Instructions

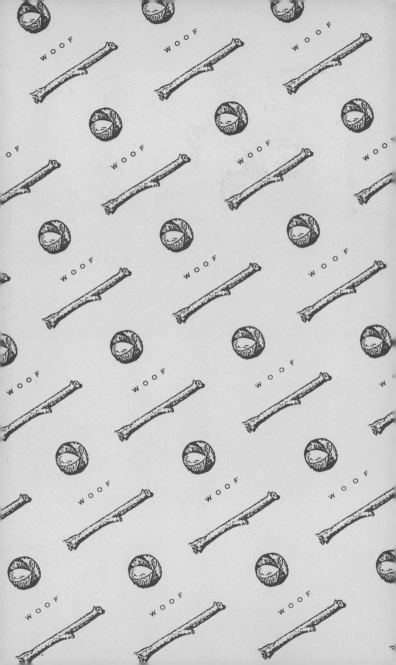